# 40,000 FORDS

## HOW TO RECESSION PROOF YOUR BUSINESS

A SUCCESSFUL BUSINESS MODEL FOR SELLING
CARS ONE AT A TIME

Fred Vollmer

40,000 FORDS
Copyright © 2011 by Fred Vollmer

ISBN 0615620663

## Dedication

**Thank you Lela for being my life long partner.**

# TABLE OF CONTENTS

.

.

# Preface

This book encompasses close to thirty years of selling cars, especially Fords.

When I started my career, I worked briefly at the Ford assembly plant in St. Louis and was in training to be a production supervisor.

Production was not for me and I went to Ford Marketing Corporation, a division of Ford Motor Company. During that time, I ordered, scheduled, distributed, and sold new vehicles to and for Ford dealers in Missouri, Illinois, and Texas.

I left Ford and worked in sales for Ford dealers and eventually became a Ford dealer.

Because of my factory background, I prided myself on selling Fords in volume therefore selling over 40,000 Fords in my career.

This book was written to assist factory personnel, car sales management, and automobile dealers to sell more vehicles.

It is also intended to give an insight to the car business to the general public.

## Introduction

The goal of this book is to entertain and educate. The car business intrigues a lot of people. Other than a house, an automobile is the second largest purchase made by the average household.

The automobile business is both seasonal and cyclical. It generally represents free enterprise as it is one of the few businesses that often includes a trade and the price is generally negotiated.

A lot has changed in the last 30 years, but a lot has remained the same.

This book has been written to read fast with each chapter containing ideas, thoughts and practices that have not only worked for me but for many in the industry.

I hope you have fun with the book and prosperity follows you wherever you go.

.

CHAPTER 1

WHAT IT TAKES TO CONQUER A RECESSION AND TURN AROUND A GOOD STORE.

It was January of 1983. I just landed an opportunity to become a partner at what I thought was one of the best potential Ford dealerships in the United States. It was in St. Louis, Missouri and the area had gone through one of the deepest recessions ever. It had three partners who in their younger days put together a Ford powerhouse. Age, personal problems and the economy had this dealership way below its potential.

The circumstances were very good in that the dealer had cut the inventory to the bone. The sales personnel were well above average and the dealer had slashed the advertising budget. The dealership was selling 60 to 90 vehicles per month. Two years later it was selling 200 to 300 per month.

The new car/truck manager, Randy Scharf and used car manager Angelo Rizzo I felt were adequate. (Little did I know that they were among the best ever at their positions.) The F&I department needed an over haul  We needed a few more good salesmen.  We needed to increase the inventory and execute several good advertising campaigns.

To be a good new car dealership, you have to have a better used car dealership. My definition of a good new car dealership is one who outsells its competition.   Used cars are important in that one of the functions of selling new cars is being able to take their car in trade and at times value it for more than your competition. This doesn't get done unless you have a better used car department in all phases.

Because our used car department was so strong we would not hire used car salesman from the outside.  You had to sell new cars first and to be moved to the used car department if you qualified. In over 13 years at that dealership, I ran an employment ad maybe three times.

Our new car department was just as tenacious.  You bet we were high pressure in a professional nonconfrontive way.  We assumed customers were here to buy cars, not to go to a movie. They never left mad.  And if they left with a price, it was very, very low.  Real monthly closing ratios were 30 to 35 percent.

You have to be willing to work harder, smarter, and be more aggressive than your competition.  We would work deals way past closing, were open extended hours and even had Sunday sales. Keep in mind that Ford had over dealered this area and it seemed like there was a Ford dealer on every corner

At our peak we were the 34th largest Ford dealer in the United States out of over 5,000.   We won Ford's Distinguished Achievement Award practically annually.

Financing plays an integral part in the dealership.  It is a huge profit center, but just as important is the function of getting the deal bought.  We had the best finance managers because we had the best sales managers.  Even I'll take some credit here because our credit source, Ford Motor Credit knew that if there was a breath of life in a deal, we would find it!  And none of us were beyond bringing it to their attention.

Eventually Ford came out with the Escort, the Taurus, and the Explorer.  It was our job to make sure we got more than our fair share of these hot vehicles.  How do you do this?  By selling the cold ones and building a well trained and educated sales force.

# CHAPTER 2

DID I BUY A CAR?

Dear Mr. Dealer;


We visited your dealership last Friday. We met our salesman on the lot. He said he was taking a smoke break after a dull sales meeting. It was 10 AM. He was waiting for his first up.

We got out of or car and he approached us and said, "Can I help ya?" We said we were, " just looking." He said, "I'll help you look." We said, "OK."

He took us to the lot and landed us on a car after several qualifying questions. One of which was, "How many repos have you had. The finance company allows two."

He slammed us into a four door Focus after taking us on a demo drive. He even made me get into the trunk to show how much space it had.

He asked if I had a trade. He looked at it and said that the old sled was worth about five back of rough book taking into account the bender and the hail damage. He asked if I had already spent my insurance check.

We were TO'd four times by different closers. They kept going back and forth trying to bust me. There was a sign in the manager's office that said "Nobody walks till the boss talks." Finally we agreed on a deal. The salesman told me we had to visit the finance man where he would trip us and butter nose the trade. We had a FICO score of 388 and only 5 19's on our bureau. We went in at full pop plus $500 on a two year lease where they were stealing our car by a grand.  It would be a done deal if we had a coX.

He told us they spotted everyone.  The car was in make ready.  We were told to get the things out of our car and that we could take the new car home.

I have just one question, "DID I BUY A CAR?"

■■■■■■■■■■■■■■■■■■■■■■■■■■■■■■■■■■■■■■■■■■■■■■■■■■■■■■■■■■

Most industries have their own slang and technical language.  This is some of ours on a slow day.

# CHAPTER 3

## MIDNIGHT MEMOS

I worked for a brief time in North Dallas, Texas with a guy named Ric Middlekauff. Ric was from California and he owned a Ford dealership that was financed partially by the factory. Ford's version was Dealer Development. GM's version was Motors Holding.

Ric had a great personality and a true spirit and knowledge of how to sell cars. He was young, wore Polo shirts and smoked Dunhill cigars. If anyone ever belonged in Dallas, it was him.

The country was in its second energy crisis and interest rates were approaching record highs. This was 1981. When I decided to write this book, I wrote a list of chapters and topics I wanted to discuss. Midnight Memos was a topic I chose. After I listed the topics, I think the Today show had a time management guru that talked about things to do when you couldn't sleep. Among them was writing.

Ric had his plate full. He was in the middle of one of the wealthiest areas in Texas where BMW's ruled, not Fords. He was on a shoe string budget with a secretary treasurer who allegedly was stealing and many of his salesmen were on drugs. To my dismay, we even made the front page of the Dallas Morning News when Nancy Reagan came to town with one of the biggest drug busts in history.

We should have known. When you have a finance manager wearing sunglasses all day and when he does take them off his pupils looked like a sharp pencil, there might be a problem.

In my opinion Ric as me was totally blindsided by the situation. Drug testing was not a normal occurrence back then.

Ric used to write rather long memorandums at night probably because he couldn't sleep. He called them Midnight Memos. Maybe I'll steal the name and use it as a title for a blog.

# CHAPTER 4

## BE CAREFUL OUT THERE

There are risks you take everyday. Here are three of them that are particularly interesting. Keep these in mind as you pursue your daily chores.

The first is watch out for vehicles backing up. You can always look the driver in the eyes to make sure they are aware of your presence when you are in front of a moving vehicle. A good dealer friend of mine was hospitalized after he was run over by a car going in reverse. His legs were broken as he was going between two vehicles.

I was at one dealership when a customer came in to pick up his vehicle from the body shop. The customer asked if he could drive the car to make sure it was fixed. We sent a technician along to make sure the customer's concerns were properly addressed. At the first stoplight, the customer pulled out a gun and said "This is where you get out." Wisely, the technician obliged and walked back to the dealership.

To properly appraise a vehicle, it must be driven. The used car manager mounted a 2000 Harley Low Rider, released the clutch and drove off a 10 foot retaining wall totaling the Harley and breaking a leg and an arm.

We deal with moving objects every day. As soon as you drop your guard something weird is going to happen. I guess it is just part of life.

# CHAPTER 5

PAY BY YHE BREAK

We were having a lot of night problems.  Mirrors and bumpers were frequently stolen off trucks.  Vehicles were being vandalized and stolen. In the car business productivity is ruled by pay plans.  Ric came up with a unique incentive he called pay by the break.  He hired two off duty policemen who had reputations of being tough, to watch our lot at night. The pay plan was hourly plus $100 per break.  Break an arm…that's $100.  Break a leg….that's another $100.

Just the word on the street stopped the damage and theft immediately.  Just for the record, no one was ever harmed.

CHAPTER 6

MEETINGS

1.  The Sales Meeting

This is another section that could be a book.  If you are in sales, to me it is the most important meeting there is be it bad or good.  It is the thread of organization.  I used to have them daily.  Sales meetings were always positive, hopefully inspirational, and educational.

Most organizations have a daily sales board with some kind of objective and performance.  Most of them are monthly.  I personally do not think it should be public.  I kept mine in a sales office where it was readily available to other sales personnel and managers.

It is nice if you can have a dedicated room for special meetings.  On the wall should be positive quotes or inspirational pictures.

2.  The Staff Meeting

Depending on the size of the dealership this should be done daily or weekly as an organizational tool.  It seems during the daily routine all departments get caught up in their own daily schedules.  Coordination between departments is a must.  This is the best way to do it.

One of the best is a weekly lunch meeting at a local restaurant. It takes you away from business and gives you a time to get together and iron out problems.

3. The Advertising meeting

John Bearce in Peoria, Illinois used to be one of the most organized dealers I have met. He meetings his people to death, but he had fantastic results. Every Monday after his daily staff meeting he would hold an advertising meeting with his department managers and his advertising agency.

They would go over the month's budget comparing planned to actual and make adjustments. It is real easy for your advertising budget to get "out of whack" if is not watched closely.

# CHAPTER 7

ALTERNATIVE FUELS, GAS PRICES AND ELECTRIC CARS

It's hard to believe that roughly 30 years ago there were sudden gas shortages in the world. This shortage seemed to be a little more drastic than the one we have now in that it caused lines at the fuel pumps that represented a true shortage. This was roughly 1975 through 1979.

Ford, GM, and Chrysler were making cars Americans wanted. They were big, roomy and comfortable. Gas mileage was of no concern. The government in its infinite wisdom even put requirements on emissions to mandate cleaner air. The technology just wasn't there. To get cleaner air, manufacturers used catalytic converters and mechanical schemes that choked engines instead of allowing them to breathe free.

Clean air came at the expense of fuel economy at a time when fuel economy was drastically needed.

Japanese and Korean cars were just coming into vogue especially in metropolitan areas. These cars were mainly an extension of the types of cars they used in Japan and Korea. Take into account the labor advantages and they were sitting on real winners. It is amazing it took them this long to make inroads into the United States.

CAFÉ. Corporate Average Fuel Economy was mandated by congress. So here you have it. Congress wants to get into the car business. Engines are choked due to pollution standards at a time when there is a fuel crisis. Yet they are mandating better fuel economy.

In 1978 I was a sales manager for a highly respected dealer in Austin, Texas, Leif Johnson Ford. A local entrepreneur had gotten a grant from the government for a few million dollars to build electric cars. They took new Escorts and removed the engines and transmissions and replaced them with batteries.

There were incentives for businesses to accommodate electric cars by placing external outlets to plug them in to charge while their employees were at work. The cars had a cruising range of 35 to 50 miles and could go 50 to 60 miles per hour on the highway. They were roughly $1500 to $2000 more expensive than a gas car. Texas Instruments even built special plugs in their parking lot for the flood of electric cars soon to come.

We were the national distributors for this car. Leif was a very prominent and well respected Ford dealer which made the introduction rather successful. However gas prices came down and supplies increased and made this project in my opinion a failure. This could have been the beginning of the high dollar golf cart.

# CHAPTER 8

## CHANGE IS NOT POPULAR

St. Louis and the Midwest were hit had by the recession in the late 70's and early 80's. Kribs Ford City was a well known Ford dealership in St. Louis that was especially hurt because of some internal and family problems. It presented quite an opportunity to me because I was not familiar with them and still had a positive attitude toward change.

The dealer had cut the advertising budget and the inventory to the bone. In these situations you have to act fast and be willing to make changes which included an aggressive posture.

The Ford dealers had become a cluster of good old boys and most of the dealers had assumed their roles. There was no price fixing or collusion, but in groups sometimes it is difficult to break away from the status quo. Jack Kribs, my partner and managing owner had severe health problems. When I took over it required a more aggressive platform to move the needle. Needless to say, the other dealers did not like the new boy in town. And Jack took numerous calls concerning our pricing and advertising.

A neighboring dealer used to wait for my ad to run and then copy it and run an exact copy with his name on it.

For several years there has been a St. Louis Automotive Dealers auto show usually near the end of January. Hundreds of cars are sold at this show. Sales personnel are allocated from the various member dealers to work the show.

I had received a call that the show was extremely successful and the sales personnel manning the show need some help, so I took four additional salesmen down to work it. Shortly I was called to a hallway and surrounded by three other dealers and told to get my men out of the show.    After some arguing I left and took the added personnel with me and signed a deal on the way out.

# CHAPTER 9

A $100,000 PLUS IDEA

Depending on how you implement it, this is probably the most consistent traffic generator I have ever seen and is mostly plus business. I call it the Super Sunday Sale. I saw it over 20 years ago and have used it effectively where ever I have gone. It makes sense and is cheap.

Consistency, desire, organization and hard work, makes this idea work. You have to realize that you have a 24 hour seven day a week selling environment  To work the plan the way I like to work it, you have to be in a market that is closed on Sundays. Twenty four hour markets are tough, but I would find a special time and try to market that.

Another great feature of the Super Sunday Sale is that a large number of people do not want to talk to a salesman and want space. If given that space with the right environment, they will buy from you.

Shop Sunday, Buy Monday. No Salesmen. No Hassle. Prices clearly marked on over 500 vehicles.

The above phrases are magic and if properly executed will give you a free days worth of sales a month. In our case that would be $260,000 worth of sales per year.

If you are a dealer or sales manager and have bought this book, borrowed this book, or found it in the bathroom and read the above paragraphs, put a plan of action to use this simple technique today.

I can't emphasize enough how important it is to maintain a competitive attitude within an organization. It should begin within the highest realm of management and directed down the chain of command. There is no substitute for hard work and being willing to do things others do not want to do.

The Super Sunday Sale is a concept of being willing to work harder and find more time to produce incremental sales. People enjoy and demand time off. If not presented in a motivational atmosphere many sales personnel will not enthusiastically embrace working extra hours.

This may not be a big problem in the Super Sunday Sale concept. But it is a big deal during Sale A Thons and Midnight or All Night Sales.

We only have 24 hours in a day. Using them wisely and creating a "sale" atmosphere at all times is important. Since most vehicle purchases are want purchases vs. need purchases, many buyers need to have a reason to buy today.

Most people genuinely want to help others succeed. If a dealer or salesman is in a contest of some type simply disclosing that to the customer can help close a deal.

For over 25years I have tried to inspire salesmen and sales managers to go the extra mile to be successful. Another thing to do is put business cards under the windshield wipers of vehicles when the dealership is closed. Yet very seldom is it done.

Another variation of the weekend sale especially in used cars is the bid box. Simply make a bid box and place empty bid sheets on your cars or lot. Mark your cars with a special price. If that isn't low enough, ask for bids. Make sure the bid sheet has name and phone number blanks.

Call everyone the next day that bid on the vehicle and try to make a deal! I've sold over 50 vehicles on a Monday with this sale. Trust me, it works.

.

## CHAPTER 10

## STEAL GOOD IDEAS

I don't think I have ever come up with an original idea. But why should I when I have thousands of others to do it for me. When I am out of town, I get competitive news papers. I talk to every salesman who approaches me with ideas instead of throwing them out the dealership. I buy most ad clipping services and constantly am on the prowl for new ideas including every media possible.

I like sales trainers and motivational speakers. I welcome my Ford rep and pick his brain for new ideas.

Direct mail is the best bang for the buck.

I've seen some great creative ad campaigns wasted with poor execution.

My main goal was to get traffic into the store. If I did that my sales force could handle the rest.

CHAPTER 11

ADVERTISING FOR SUCCESS

In the car business, advertising is a necessary evil. There are college courses and hundreds of books written on the subject. It has the satisfaction coefficient of Picasso finishing a painting or Dickens finishing a novel. There is a rush in successful creativity. Nothing is more fun than a successful ad campaign or promotion.

There are two ends of the retail automotive spectrum. One end is volume, the other end is gross. Both represent profit depending how well you can get the two to work together.

I like event advertising which I will discuss later. To get your message heard I feel it is important to dominate a local media. A few of the media options are newspaper, direct mail, radio, television, the internet, flyers, etc. Obviously it would be cool to be able to buy 24 hours of television time on all stations, but this isn't practical. One needs to set an objective and set a budget. The success of the sale then depends on the creativity, closing abilities, and quality of the traffic.

Which ever media you pick, be the best at it and throw your main focus into it using the others to back up and support your main thrust.    The two most used media are television and newspaper.    Experienced dealers and advertising reps can argue about the merits of both forever.    But which ever you like, dominate it to the best of your ability and support it with one or two of the others maybe using a 70-15-15 percent ratio.

Creativity plays such a big roll in the success of a promotion.  I spend a lot of time reading and researching.  I looked and talked to every person who came into the dealership with an idea looking for a new edge.  Many successful dealers fly by the seat of their pants looking for that promotion that will bring them a pot of gold.

# CHAPTER 12

## HOW TO DOMINATE A MARKET FOR HALF WHAT OTHERS PAY

In our own way, we are all egotistical. Being a good negotiator is a big asset. Two great tools for negotiation are money and courtesy mixed with respect. Obtaining dominance on a shoestring might be the name of my next book. But the secret has already been expressed.

Courtesy mixed with respect is probably not something you can learn but should be aware of. In every media there are special events, special times, and special offers. There are also hierarchies to deal with i.e. salesman, sales manager, general manager, and owner. Each one of them has their own little space. But most of them want the job done from the bottom up. Even the little guy has power. If he likes and respects you and knows you have the money to pay for it--You Win. Given average creativity and average closing ratios, you have just out marketed your opponent.

Meet the media representative regularly and always ask them for a deal. Keep abreast of what is new. Ask them what you need to do to get on page one instead of three. What new inserts are coming out? Sooner or later they will tell you. But you constantly need to be probing and asking questions.

..

# CHAPTER 13


## EVENTS CAN MAKE A DIFFERENCE


Event advertising has always been successful for me. Of course you have winners and losers, but the long term effect has been well worth it. The car business runs in monthly cycles.

The month starts off and there are zero units sold. Normally annual, monthly, weekly and even daily objectives are set. The factory has several promotions a year. Most of them do not seem to be well planned. Most of them are reactionary to the market and what other manufacturers are doing. Such things as rebates and interest rate buy downs often come as a surprise.

Event promotions along with dominate and creative advertising plus good timing can make the difference in a month or a year! Such things as Red Tag Sales, Mustang Stampede, Car Wars, and hundreds of others work if planned and executed properly.

Excitement runs through the whole dealership. Excitement, enthusiasm, and confidence sell cars or for that matter anything.

CHAPTER 14

THE TELEPHONE

The telephone is an amazing communication device. I bet Alexander Graham Bell would love to see what has happened to his invention.

Rather than get into a telephone seminar, there are just a few points I would like to make about the telephone and car dealerships.

The department that normally gets the most phone calls is the parts department, followed up by the service department. Then it is the vehicle sales department.

It is wise to keep a phone log especially to track calls when ever you have a promotion or advertising campaign. The purpose of most advertising campaigns it to generate traffic. People like to let their fingers do the walking. Thousands of dollars are spent on just publicizing numbers in yellow pages and other advertising vehicles.

When someone walks into your showroom, you wish your best salesmen could be cloned and handle the prospect. Unfortunately that doesn't usually happen. The same is with the telephone. I want my best telephone person to handle the phone call.

All calls should be handled in a friendly and courteous manner. But there is only one way to handle an incoming call for a prospective car buyer and that is GET THEIR NAME AND NUMBER AND CALL THEM BACK! Use any excuse you want, but getting their name and number should be the primary objective.

Once you have gotten their name and number it is OK to sell all you can, but your NEXT main objective is to SELL AN APPOINTMENT.

Very seldom are cars sold over the phone and almost never to a cold call phone up.

# CHAPTER 15

## HOW TO MAINTAIN CUSTOMER SATISFACTION

Several years ago the factories tied customer satisfaction ranking into most of their award programs. Then they wanted to show they were serious and tied it into traditional holdbacks. The guy who made out like a bandit was/is the measurer, J. D. Powers.

Dealers risk millions of dollars in the car arena. The factories MBA's risk their careers and with their youthful exuberance tell dealers how to run their business. Absolutely they have some good ideas and programs, but more and more factory personnel are out of touch with the internal mechanisms that run their dealership brands, the salesmen, managers, mechanics, and the dealers. When something goes wrong the customer is hurt the most, followed by the dealer and to some extent the factory.

The profit incentive, the golden rule and common sense makes most business men critically aware of customer satisfaction. Most dealers I know give customer satisfaction with their heart and good business sense, not with factory incentives.

It is a shame that generally factory people have not received letters of thanks from a happy buyer or a customer whose problem was fixed in the dealer's shop.

Nor have they had the great feelings when you get a picture from a customer's son to whom you donated a scholarship or money to certain events.

Customer satisfaction means satisfying customers. That only requires knowledge, reasonableness, and to some extent money. The factory, rightfully so, wants to keep the dealer at the forefront. Yet there are times when just the presence of a factory rep can really help. The problem is that most factory representatives are scared to death to face an irate customer one on one. I really do not blame them because irate customers, other than loosing money, are the least fun part of the deal.

Nobody wants to deal with upset customers. We used to call them heat cases. You can feel a heat case when they walk in the door. That is why most dealers' offices have two doors, one to enter in and the other to escape.

I have a friend that is a very successful insurance agent. He and his three sons run one of the largest independent agencies in the United States. He works three hours a day and nicknames himself, "the fireman." He tells the kids to give him the heat! All he cares about is problems and upset customers. And he handles them one on one until the customer is satisfied or there is no where else to go.

I was the managing partner and general sales manager for two top 100 Ford dealers for over 15 years. I have been responsible for a lot of retail sales. We sold retail and we sold clean. I have never been in a court room defending an awkward sale.

First of all, you have to know you have a problem. Then you need to do what it takes to resolve it. Most times you meet in the middle. But even if you loose, it still was cheaper than next week's ad budget.

# CHAPTER 16

## LEASING VS. BUYING

Leasing has been a financial vehicle that can be your best friend or worst enemy. It is a method of financing that uses leverage to its maximum. Other than cash down, leasing dramatically reduces payments because the residual reduces the finance balance. In the hands of an unscrupulous greedy individual, the profit can be obscene.

Once a client is convinced that leasing is the way to go, margins and profit can be very high because most individuals are comparing a lease payment to a buy payment. Also cash down in a lease has a much greater effect on the payment than it does on a buy because the cash down represents a much greater percentage of the finance balance therefore making the payment less.

Comparing a lease payment to a buy payment is like comparing buying a car to a wheel barrow. In stock market vernacular, it is like buying futures compared to the stock.

Most people are payment buyers. That is they want the most vehicle they can get for a predetermined monthly amount in their monthly budget. Figure the payment along with the down payment and this represents the total outlay for their vehicle.

In today's world management and salesmen must be well versed in leasing because of the leverage it provides. It is perfectly reasonable for people to lease because they can drive so much more for so much less.

# CHAPTER 17

## WHAT IS AN OBSCENE PROFIT?

We are not children here, but what is a fair profit? Many car deals represent a confrontational battle with the client wanting to buy a car at the lowest possible price and the dealer wanting the highest price. Somewhere in the middle there is a meeting of the minds and a final price is determined. In my opinion one side of the problem stems from industry pay plans that are based on percentage of profit rewarding salesmen, sales managers, finance managers, and eventually the dealer based on the American tradition of making money.

That is partially why the industry has such a bad reputation. Most people do not want to negotiate, but they want your best price. They buy a car and as soon as they get home they show it to their neighbor. It may not be the first question out of his mouth, but sooner or later he is going to want to know what kind of "deal" you got.

CHAPTER 18

THE ECONOMICS OF A CAR DEAL

In many situations it is difficult to tell who is in charge of approving a deal. It could be the dealer himself, an appointed manager or the salesman. But all car deals are figured the same way. I have worked over 20,000 deals and it all comes down to one thing, profit.

It is a simple mathematic equation but sometimes it takes a long time to get there. But the bottom line is a simple accounting T. How much is coming in versus how much is going out. The list can be endless but examples of things coming in are cash down, rebates, dealer incentives, trade equity, finance balance, and more. The list going out can be just as cumbersome such as the cost of the car, options, payoffs, inspections, rebates, insurance, negative down payments, and more.

Subtract what is going out against what is coming in and if it is positive than you have a profit. Negative is a loss. Both can be acceptable or unacceptable. The profit may not be enough to make an acceptable deal. And the loss may be the way to go. That's right. Good dealers take losses.

CHAPTER 19

## ASK FOR LETTERS OF REFERENCE

I used to feel that if I did a good job and made customers happy that the reward would take care of itself.   Maybe that was true years ago, and maybe it still is, but sometimes even customers do not know if they are happy or not.

Many dealers think that factory people walk around with their head in the clouds, having never had the pressure to make a living using the profit motive.   They do not have the pressure of making a payroll or rent payment.

Many factory people think that dealers are a bunch of spoiled hayseeds.  If it weren't for them the dealers wouldn't be around. The factory comes up with all kinds of ridiculous programs that it forces the dealers to buy.   One program that is not ridiculous, but has unbelievable consequences was Blue Oval.

It started out several years ago as a satisfaction questionnaire. All manufactures are rated by J.D. Powers' surveys and ranked accordingly.   This is big business as the ratings are highly publicized and have an effect on the buying public.

The questionnaires are divided so one can tell which department and even to some extent which personnel were helping or hurting the score.  There are big time bonuses for high scores and big time penalties for low scores.  So big time you could even face termination as a dealer for low scores. Dealers made changes in their organizations to accommodate the questionnaire.   Some paid customers to bring in the survey and if the numbers were acceptable, they would get a gift or a free oil change.

I used to keep a scrapbook in the service waiting area called "Nice Notes from Nice Folks" that contained letters from happy customers. I used to have my salesmen solicit them from happy customers and keep their own brag book. The customers didn't mind. They actually went out of their way to send some very nice letters. This was not only good to make people aware that the dealer cared, but helped customer satisfaction ratings.

# CHAPTER 20

## WRITING DOWN AGED INVENTORY

Normally a vehicle brings its highest value the day it hits the lot ready to be sold.

No one likes to take a loss on a sale. There is an old adage in the car business that states your first loss is your best loss. In most circumstances that is true.

Managers really hate to take losses, but it is a necessary evil in the car business especially used cars.

As inventory gets older it depreciates, especially used cars. A car today is worth more that a car tomorrow. The ideal goal is to own every car in your inventory at a price where they can be easily disposed or wholesaled with no loss or gain. If you have a gain in your used car inventory then you are probably missing business.

The best way to adjust your inventory is to periodically write it down or reduce it. Most dealers set up an account when they acquire it especially if it is purchased from an outside source such as auctions. They set up reserves for a percentage of the cost or a fixed amount. When a vehicle hits a certain age say 30, 60, 90 days they adjust its value and write it down.

In real estate the biggest reason a property doesn't sell is because it is priced too high. It is amazing how much condition and cleanliness can increase value in both real estate and vehicles.

I THINK YOU WILL FIND THAT USED CAR LOSSES ARE MORE DUE TO LACK OF CONDITIONING AND CLEANLINESS THAN BEING OVER PRICED.

At the end of the year if the account is too high take some of the excess and have a party or some reward.  Or you can just take it into profit.

CHAPTER 21

THE GOLDEN MOMENT--DELIVERING THE VEHICLE

The sale of a vehicle can sometimes be quite a battle. But generally once a particular vehicle has been selected by the consumer and a price has been negotiated, most of the hostility has been released. Most buyers are anxious to get the process over with and take their new purchase home. Many salesmen want to get their sale delivered and go find another customer.

As a salesman there should be a lot of pride and concern at the delivery of the vehicle. There is pride in having closed a sale. And concern in getting the vehicle delivered as smoothly as possible. A lot can happen between the acceptance of the deal and the delivery of the vehicle. During this time the buyer is vulnerable because most of the time they feel the battle is over.

It is during this time when important aftermarket products are presented. Such things as credit life, protective products, warranties, anti theft products and more are sold to the new buyers usually by another sales specialist. The profits in this department can be substantial depending on the philosophy of the dealer and the ability of the aftermarket sales specialist.

There are as many different delivery processes as there are dealers, but generally the buyer expects a clean new car that works. Assuming there has already been an agreement on a particular vehicle, it is important that the customer takes possession as soon as possible.

This might seem like common sense and it is, but you would be surprised at the bureaucracy that still exists to get the car ready for delivery. It can be a supposedly simple clean up to installing and applying aftermarket products like radios, remote starters, sealants, etc. Remember until the car is delivered something bad can happen!

The most important guy in the dealership is the wash attendant or porter. Nothing but nothing is worse than delivering a dirty vehicle. These guys rule the dealership and often hold salesmen hostage waiting for the vehicle to be cleaned up and serviced. The teamwork in this department is paramount for customer satisfaction.

As a salesman there is always that uncertainty in the back of his mind until the vehicle is gone i.e." over the curb."

# CHAPTER 22

## WHY IT IS IMPORTANT TO BE THE USED CAR KING.

Trading is the name of the game if you want a successful car dealership. Close to 80% of new and used vehicle deals have trades involved. Not only must you dispose of the trade but you must generally pay the highest price for it.

Generally the dealer who can give the highest price for the trade will get the deal. First of all you need a dedicated, honest used car manager. It is a shame that the nature of our business includes theft awareness. Many things can be hidden in the used car department. Probably the biggest fear among experienced dealers is an "under the table payment" to a used car manager from a wholesale buyer. On the other hand I have heard of dealers requiring "under the table payments" to themselves from wholesalers for every car sold.

When working a car deal there is no better feeling than selling a car to an individual who has shopped an entire city and making the decision to purchase from you. This book is about that, but a big part of the deal is the perception that the buyer received a fair value for their trade.

I personally like the new vehicle sales function over the used. But to be a successful new car dealer, you must be a successful used car dealer.

To me it was so important that all my used car salesmen had to be promoted to the used car department after being in new cars. In another section I discuss the importance of getting good salesmen. I believe in the golden rule. I treat people well and pay the best. In return, I expect the best.

CHAPTER 23

## WHY SHOULD I HAVE A 30 DAY, 60 DAY, 90 DAY, 120 DAY 150 DAY, 180 DAY RULE?

"The money is in the used car department." That is another reason to be the used car king. CASH!! Normally when a vehicle is traded for, it represents a significant part of the dealer's cash. Later on I'll discuss the "float," but for now I'll stay on the philosophy of turning, valuing, advertising, SELLING, vehicles within a certain time period more lovingly known as aged units.

What is really neat about car dealers is they wear so many different hats and you can have several profit centers. Normally each profit center functions on how important the dealer feels it is and the manager involved. For example if the dealer is really excited about the parts department, normally it will excel. But if parts really don't turn him on and he has an exceptional manager, parts can also do well.

Many dealers are simply money managers. That is obviously one of the best traits to have. But there is still a place for a "car guy," someone who knows and likes to trade cars. Every dealer has a philosophy about aged used cars and even identical twins do not agree. Any dealer who does not manage aged used cars will not be a dealer for very long. AGED USED CARS REPRESENT THE BIGGEST DRAIN ON A NEW CAR OR USED CAR DEALER. This is probably the number one expense in the car industry.

What is even worse is that by the time you realize you are out of whack, at the least, it is going to hurt and can even be too late.

But a car guy dealer is my kind of dealer. This is a risk taker who can feel the success of a car line or a particular car. Cars are like people. They all have different personalities. Some you love. Some you like. Some you hate. And some you don't even know. The worst is the last. The one you do not know. That is the one through laziness, ignorance, and lack of attention sticks around and costs you money instead of making money.

I do not care if you sell 1,000 used cars a month or 10, if someone is not in control of reconditioning, advertising, desking deals, and monitoring salesmen, you will have a used car problem.

Aged used car problems are like cancer. If you do not nip it in the bud, it spreads. Good car salesmen are like hawks. Since most of them are paid on commission, the good salesmen will take advantage of cars that are not bid properly. If a trade is bid too high, they will walk around it. If too low, it flies out the door.

The bottom line is that it really doesn't matter as much what you do, as long as you do something.

.

# CHAPTER 24

## HOW TO APPRAISE A USED CAR

I have tried to dwell on what I feel are more advanced and technical things I have picked up in managing, owning and visiting car dealers. I've looked for solutions and pitfalls rather than basics. What is amusing is that there have been great changes in retailing, but there are still basics that haven't really changed. For example, gas prices went wild in the 70's with two crises. Car gluts and the anticipation of Japanese cars taking over the U.S. were predicted 20 years ago.

The greatest change in the used car business is the constant change and addition of consumer regulations. When you appraise a car, you are expected to know if it has been wrecked or modified. You are the expert. Any representation of a vehicle by a consumer had better be documented and even signed. As a dealer, you are the expert. If a customer tells you his trade has not been wrecked or had hail damage and in fact it has. You believe him and give him full value for the car. Sell it to another party and if you do not have documentation, baby, YOU ARE A LOOSER.

You are the expert!

CHAPTER 25


ONE ON ONE WITH THE FACTORY

Moving from wholesale to retail was a big decision for me. I got my dream job with Ford Motor Company after I was discharged from the Army. At that time is was one of the largest companies in the world. I had an MBA and started at to me was a fantastic salary.

I started in St. Louis and was transferred to Houston, Texas. Texas Ford dealers as a group were very profitable and they we gong through a growth cycle. My job was to wholesale vehicles from Ford to Ford dealers. This part of the distribution process has changed immensely through the years because of law suits by dealers to manufacturers. For awhile it was easier to make money suing the manufacturer for distribution practices than selling cars.

We would also coordinate marketing plans between the factory and the dealer. I used to laughingly call it selling "trinkets.' There were such things as showroom introduction materials, parts truck decals, and a host of other special programs. My favorite was Punt, Pass, and Kick and is still used by the National Football League. We were not commissioned, but your future depended on getting dealers to sign up and participate in these programs. I used to call it a franchise tax.

Car dealers are a special breed. By nature they are optimistic and risk takers. When I moved to the retail side of the business I bought it all. And for doing that I would get a special favor every once in awhile. The factory had been good to me and although some of the programs seemed ridiculous, it usually paid to go along with them

But if you are a dealer as with anything in life, you can be bitten and bitten hard with consequences that can be as dire and putting you out of business.

One such product was a computer system initially sold by Ford to Ford dealers.  It was an expensive item that required long term maintenance.  Ford spun the computer company off and it became a separate entity.  For me the deal never worked out.

# CHAPTER 26

## WHY PANNING VOLUME IS IMPORTANT

In a new car franchise planning volume is the amount of new vehicles the factory feels a particular dealer should sell to represent them in a market. This is my own definition, not necessarily theirs.

I guess as a former "factory man" this kind of gave me an expectation as to how big the dealer was or was supposed to be. It also gave me some sort of guide line of how many units to expect the dealership to sell. This was important as to buying, selling, or consulting a particular dealership.

Planning volumes change as markets change. The addition or subtraction of dealers in a market would mean the addition or subtraction of planning volume. This can be important for factory contests, incentives, and awards.

You should always know what the factory expects and how you measure up to that expectation. You should document well any correspondence or meeting with factory representatives concerning any matters of expectations and requirements to stay on good standing.

# CHAPTER 27

HOW TO GET YOUR FAIR SHARE OF NEW VEHICLES WITHOUT GETTING BURRIED IN SLOW MERCHANDISE

I spent my first couple of years at Ford in the distribution department. I was lucky because there were two of us starting at the same time and the other guy got the mail room. Back then a dealer would order each car on a form and mail it to the district. Clerks and a new machine "a computer" would scan the form and make sure it was a buildable unit. Approximately 70% of the orders from dealers could not be built as they ordered them.

One such order was a 1973 Cinnamon Fire Thunderbird with a blue interior. We deviated the spec and built it. The dealer refused it and Sherwood Ford along with 10 Pintos bought it.

Dealers were allocated production monthly based on several factors (sales history, planning volume, others) and how many units the factory could build. Allocating vehicles is a touchy subject as dealers have won millions of dollars from the factory because of the economic consequences of not having vehicles to sell.

Back in the late '40's and early '50's stories are told that when a truck load of vehicles was delivered to a dealership a factory rep would be there to get one free as a favor for getting the dealer the other five or six. I'm sure this is not true, but who knows?

Also dealers have lost millions of dollars in excessive floor plan costs because of sloppy ordering and not watching order banks. Over 80% of Ford dealers offered this book could pay for it in 5 minutes if they read and understand the above sentence.

If you are a dealer or sales manager and you are not 100% confident in the integrity of your order bank, you should immediately check it and make sure you are not over ordered in unwanted vehicles and under ordered in wanted vehicles.

Good sales managers are not necessarily shirking their duties by not having order banks up to par. Ordering cars is tough but most sales managers also have individuals (salesmen) to manage. Both jobs are incredibly important.

# CHAPTER 28

## THE SALES, STOCK , AND PRODUCTION RUNDOWN

In ordering a well planned inventory, this is the most important document, concept or formula that is available. The factory uses this to determine "fair share" production. Many dealers have received huge settlements because of court decisions based on unfair distribution practices.

In a perfect world the factory can build inventory to meet market demands on a timely basis. In the real world it is an expensive guessing game that depends on many many variables.

It is up to the dealer to sell the factory as to why he wants more vehicles than are available. It can also be used as a defense as to why a dealer would decline a vehicle order.

Management needs to put together a plan as to how many vehicles it wants. I like to do it at least weekly and monthly and compare it to the factory's offer. I used to consider their offer fiction. It is the dealer's responsibility to tell the manufacturer why he wants or doesn't want offered merchandise. The sales, stock, and production rundown is the method to do this and serves as a record that you either refused merchandise or wanted more.

The variables are stock, projected sales, desired inventory and factory offer. A good dealer or manager should be able to do this in his sleep. It should be done by car and truck line and even be broken down to options and colors.

The factory will use their figures.  YOU MUST USE YOURS.  An axiom to use is that you can't project too low sales for cold units or too high sales for hot units.

Here is a short example for Fusion for a month:

| Stock | 4 |
| Less Projected sales | 6 |
| Balance | -2 |
| Desired Inventory | 10 |
| Need to order | 12 |
| Factory offer | 2 |
| Plus/minus | -10 |

You should keep notes of your negotiations as to why or why not you received certain merchandise.

During build out periods or plant shut downs this process gets complex but must be done at least weekly.

## CHAPTER 29

## DON'T FIX SOMETHING THAT ISN'T BROKE

How do you know when to make changes? Change is inevitable. But change for change sake can cost a lot of money. People tend to resist change unless they are brought into the decision process. Even then it may not be a success because it may not be a change for the better.

We all have resisted change at some time in our life. I have seen a lot of dealers make some ridiculous changes when the organization was flying high.

Ford used to promote from within. They have always had a place for youth. It was understood that if you weren't on a certain pace in management by 40, it was time to retire. In the early 90's the sales department changed, maybe the whole company did. They started hiring and bringing outsiders in upper management looking for new ideas. I was a dealer then and was somewhat surprised.

I have always wondered why dealers are so reluctant to do the same thing, hiring from within and building your own management and sales team. There is a lot of talent going to waste.

"Insanity is expecting different results from the same process." Obviously this is different from "don't fix something that isn't broke." I've seen just the opposite where obvious problems are over looked. If the deal isn't working, you must change it to get it working. Fix bad habits now! Do not wait until it is too late.

It is the simple things that will kill you. For example, a salesman does not get the name and number of a prospect. A manager doesn't talk to a customer walk out. The phone doesn't get answered properly. The list goes on and on.

## CHAPTER 30

## USE BEN FRANKLIN FOR MAKING DECISIONS

Ben Franklin must have been quite a guy. He gets a lot of credit for inventions, patriotism, and philosophy. I have been to several sales schools. Just about every one has them has the "Ben Franklin Close" so I thought I would make sure it was included in this book.

I have used it mostly as the Ben Franklin Close. But it is useful for just about any decision-making process. It helps you clear your mind to make a logical and profitable decision. I guess the correct term is the "right decision."

Every person should be introduced to the Ben Franklin method of making decisions. Simply put you make a T. Next you define the problem or decision you are trying to make. On one side of the T you put the positive reasons for the decision; on the other side you put the negative sides of the decision. I use a check mark for each answer. If the check marks in the positive side outnumber the negative side then the positive side should be taken. Conversely if the negative side out numbers the positive side then the negative side should be taken.

Obviously in a sales situation, the salesman could lead and help the buyer make the right decision. That is to say "yes" to buying a vehicle today.

# CHAPTER 31

## THE IMPORTANCE OF ACCURATE PAPERWORK

Leif Johnson Ford in Austin, Texas has for years been a leading Ford dealer in just about every aspect of the word. I was hired from a Field Manager position at Ford to a truck manager's position at Leif Johnson Ford in 1977. I was working in Houston, but I really was from Missouri. The Midwest was in a major recession caused by fuel shortages. It was very similar to now. Only interest rates and inflation were high.

Generally larger Texas dealers made more money than Midwest dealers because of right to work and fewer dealers per capita. The Midwest had dealers on every corner while Texas had fewer but larger dealers.

I was hired by Robert Johnson and Bob Clark. But since I traveled the Austin area for Ford I knew Leif. He was trying to retire so he wasn't at the dealership too often. Leif was also a previous factory guy, so we had a few stories in common. Robert was the GM and ran the store. Later after Bob Clark retired I became the New Vehicle Manager.

Like most dealers, cash is in the used car department. Whenever Leif wanted to make a large purchase, usually real estate, we might have to liquidate some used car inventory. This is common in the industry. The used car department is generally the most profitable department in a new car dealership.

Whenever Leif was upset, Robert always took the heat. We had a sales meeting every morning at 9 AM. The only one Leif ever attended while I was there was to stress the importance of getting deals properly documented.

A large car dealership requires exceptional money management skills as balances are generally higher than a lot of businesses. Being out of trust is the greatest reason dealers go out of business.

We were one of the largest Ford dealers in Texas and the United States. We just had a floor plan check coming after a big successful sale. Deals were all over the place and Ford Credit wanted cash for every car that was not on the premises. There were over fifty deals waiting to get funded. I'm not sure but I think Leif had to make a trip to the bank.

CHAPTER 32

## CLOSING THE MONTH

There are two ends of the spectrum in selling cars. One end is purely as a means to make money. The other is the pure joy of closing a sale. Somewhere in the middle lies a reasonable position. In dealer hierarchy there are two mostly diametric sides. One is the accountant. The other is the salesman.

Car dealers and car manufacturers live month to month. Competition is fierce between brands, dealers, and salesmen. The factory wants unity among dealers, yet they put up sizable rewards and incentives for dealers who achieve higher goals.

Life used to be in 10 day periods, but those reports are no longer used. I bring them up only to make a point. Generally the first 10 days are slower than the second 10 days and the third 10 is the greatest.

I believe in event advertising. I also believe that advertising should be geared to take advantage of buyers at a time when they are in the market as opposed to trying to create a market. For example manufacturers can create markets with rebates, interest promotions, and product specials. But dealers can only get their fair share of the market the factory creates. My slogan is, 'I just want more than my fair share." You can get more than your fair share by gearing your ads during higher traffic times and the end of the month.

Getting back to the close of the month, accountants are responsible for getting a financial statement to the factory every month by the 10$^{th}$ of the following month. If the books close on the final day of the month, it is easier to get statements done in time. However, there is a lot of emotion and productivity is higher at the end of the month. In a motivated salesman's world, the month is over when the books close and it is time to go to the beach.

If there is traffic you will increase sales if you keep the books open an extra day or two. It is a matter of feel and if you are a salesman you feel it. If you are a bookkeeper, you really don't care.

Conservatively it costs a dealer 10% in sales to close his books on the exact end of the month.

CHAPTER 33


SALES SYSTEMS

Most larger dealerships use some sort of system. Hull Dobbs was the first "track house" I can remember. I never talked to them, but I met a few salesmen who worked for them.

It doesn't matter if business is good or bad. Getting qualified sales help is difficult. The car salesman has not always been one of the most enviable positions in the public eye. There are naturally talented people who can walk on the sales floor, greet a potential buyer and have his money 20 minutes.

Then there are those who will take hours walking around the lot and come up with the same result. No matter which way you look at it, the 80-20 rule seems to play out. 20% of the salesmen sell 80% of the vehicles. I strongly believe in sales training. I always paid 50% of my salesman's cost to attend sales training classes. There is a whole cottage industry of automobile sales trainers, not to mention the billions of dollars spent on general sales training in our economy.

There are a couple of philosophies involved here that hopefully melded together produce a sale. The first is what does the salesman as an individual feel he must do? The other is the system the dealer requires the salesman to perform while trying to make a sale. This is kind of hard to explain, but many salesmen try to shortcut a dealer's system.

Some dealers feel the salesman has no brain while at the other end of the spectrum some dealers let the salesman go wild. For example there is one very prominent system that requires a visit to the service department before the car is sold. If you deviate from this system step, you are subject to discipline

Life must have been pretty good in the 60's. It was not uncommon to have the salesman's office bugged with speakers to hear the conversation between the customer and the salesman. But better than that was to hear the conversation between husband and wife while the salesman was gone. That is illegal now and probably was then.

Every dealership needs to maintain some element of control over the sales process and the salesman in order to maximize profit, customer satisfaction, and organization. A sales tower is a location on the showroom floor where management can control the selling process. Sometimes it is elevated but it is always on the showroom floor.

The sales desk is in the tower if you have one. It is where the decision that a car is sold and the established price is made. If it is not in the tower, it is in the sales manager's office. Automobile sales are different from most consumer products in that prices are not set, but negotiated. The factories have been trying to get away from this concept, but trades and the law have made it tough.

.

CHAPTER 34


THE CUSTOMER BELONGS TO THE DEALER

I have a lot of respect for the retail car salesman especially the good ones who can sell for profit, sell in volume and keep customers happy. The salesman is obviously the closest link to the customer. Hopefully there is a bond built in a relationship between the customer, the salesman, and the dealership.

In most metropolitan areas different brand dealers are on the same block and same brand dealers are five miles away. Dealers are their own worst enemy in that they steal the better salesmen from each other. One such incident occurred where the salesman wanted to leave a particular dealership and asked for a record of the customers he sold. The dealer would not release them. The dealer was sued and he lost.

But what did the salesman really do? The dealer has an incredible investment in inventory, facility, advertising, service, and parts. In my opinion the dealer owns the customer and if the salesman loved his customers so much he should have had his own records.

# CHAPTER 35

## .CHANGE PAY PLANS MONTHLY

A very close friend of mine once said, "You car guys are something else. You live and die by the month." How true it is. Until recently it was closer to 10 days. I personally got demoted while at Ford for missing a 10 day number at the end of a contest period. What is really weird is that the dealer wanted desperately to win a trip. He was the largest in my zone. I was new to the zone and he told me he had 90 sales to report for the 10 day period. He came in with a 197 blowing away forecasts. There was a lot of pressure on that close. We were flying in IBM cards from all over Texas. Instead of being a hero, I was a goat because I obviously did not know what was going on in my territory.

I cannot stress enough how important this concept is to motivating an automobile sales force. It forces management to plan ahead and set objectives. It blends with the annual plan. It also allows for forgiveness for a job not so well done the month before. Or better yet to go for another record.

A good pay plan has a reward for exceptional sales performance. Salesmen love competition. You should have a general pay plan. But over and above that I always had a bonus program that involved such areas as unit sales, unit gross, aged unit sales, cold unit sales, and F&I sales (just a taste).  It could be a trip, money, or prize.

For over 25 years, every month I had a new pay plan, a new contest.  It was always based on what was most important to me.  My partners would go crazy some times, but they enjoyed the outcome.

.

## CHAPTER 36

## THE GRAND CLUB

I spent the longest six months of my life in North Dallas with Ric Middlekauff. This was retail boot camp. I came from one of the most successful Ford dealers in the United States where life was good and balanced, at least for a car guy. There was a gas crunch. Theft and drugs were a big problem. BMW's, not Ford's were in everybody's mind.

I borrowed the grand club from Ric in 1982. It is simple. It is crazy. But it is the most motivating contest I know. It has to become part of your culture. And if it is, you will not believe the results it has as a motivational factor.

Everyone would like to lead the board. Most dealers have a salesman of the month. But in a large dealership, other than your regular pay an above average month goes unrewarded.

The grand club is a private lunch with management or the dealer. Alcohol is optional. It is awarded monthly after the close of the month as soon as possible. It is important to get the prior month's business closed and get on with the new. That is just the nature of the game.

The criterion for the lunch is simple, 10 units plus a $1000 single deal. The 10 units for today is still reasonable, but I think

$1500 should be the single deal number. Whatever the number make it so at least 1/3 of your sales force can go. As a dealer or manager, you will stay in touch with your sales force.

Several years ago, I had one of my best salesmen Dave, sell 21 units without a grand hit. He led the board in volume. We had a good month and close to 80% of the sales force were at the lunch. During discussion at the lunch, the subject of Dave not being there came up. The salesmen suggested we have some sort of variance to the rules under special circumstances. When we got back to the dealership, Dave was waiting for me to tell me he was leaving and going to another dealership. (This had nothing to do with the grand club.) It was never considered again.

Think of it. For a $50 lunch, you have access in a relaxed setting to meet with your key front line people. Not only is it an award, but a time to organize and get new ideas. Everyone wants to be at the grand club.

Remember that 80% of your sales come from 20% of your salesmen. It's not the top 20% you need to worry about. It is the bottom 80%. Get them to average 10 and you will have one heck of a month.

# CHAPTER 37

## DAILY OPERATING CONTROL

It is amazing that in an industry as big as the car industry how different each dealership is from the other. But one thing the best have in common is a DOC sheet or some sort of Daily Operating Control. Generally the office manager or Secretary Treasurer keeps records comparing monthly objectives to actual performance. It is then broken down into a daily record.

Most dealers have a daily meeting to see where they stand for the month. It is broken down by department.

.

# CHAPTER 38

## THE DAILY SALES PLAN

Salesmen need some sort of direction and organization. There are productive and non productive people in any organization. The productive individuals should all have objectives of some sort. They should be measured periodically. I suggest daily. The daily sales plan does just that plus is measures daily effort.

It is a record of sales versus objectives, contacts made through phone solicitation, appointments, and follow up of walkouts.

.

# CHAPTER 39

## PROSPECTING

There a several schools of thought on prospecting.  In the car business a salesman has the obligation to the dealer to produce sales and prospects from some sort of solicitation process.  It can be personal advertising, phone solicitation, direct mail, e mail, or any other form of outside solicitation.

Some dealers feel that they are responsible for traffic and all they want are good closers and somebody there to wait on the buyers.

All I can say is if you are a good closer and you do not like prospecting, you had better be closing.

I loved Dave Sinclair.  He used to say that he didn't want his salesmen to prospect.  He would rather them read the paper.  At that time Dave was the top retail volume dealer in the country.

The death of a salesman is his failure to cultivate new business.

.

# CHAPTER 40

## EVERY SALESMAN MUST TAKE A DEMO DRIVE

Car theft in this country is unbelievable. Most police departments work hard to help local business, including car dealers. But theft is not the most important reason for going on a demonstration drive with a client, but control and qualifying are. The client is most unguarded and more likely to tell you the truth while on a demonstration drive because he is in an unfamiliar atmosphere and their subconscious makes them.

Here you will get their true feelings and factual answers on such things as down payment and payment expectations. Plus you get to know the people and are able to qualify them better.

I have always told my salesmen that if they didn't want to give a demo ride because of security to let management know and they can make a decision. I did, however, have case where we had done some body work in the body shop. We had a porter ride along with the guy as he wanted to check our work. He pulled a gun on the porter one block away and said "This is where you get out." He very smartly obeyed instructions.

.

CHAPTER 41

ATTITUDES MAKE A DIFFERENCE

You can either have a positive attitude or a negative attitude. Which ever you have depends on your outlook on life. Attitude is one facet of life over which you have some control. It doesn't matter what your rank is in an organization, your attitude spreads among the people you interact with.

The higher the rank within an organization, the more important it is to maintain a positive attitude. Let's assume the dealer is the highest ranking individual in the dealership. As he leaves home, he has an argument with his wife going out the door because his son got an F in math. He walks into the dealership and has been told there has been a car stolen last night. Sales are 30% off projection. The parts manager is sick. An irate service customer is waiting in the lobby. A commercial needs to be cut in an hour. And he has a staff meeting in five minutes.

His best salesman sees him in the lobby and says energetically, "Good morning boss! How are you doing today?" What would your answer be? The right answer is "Great." Smile and the whole world smiles with you. Cry and you cry alone. If you. the owner/manager are having a bad day, it will spread throughout the organization if you let it.

"In the car business when you get up in the morning, you have to be ready for a good fight." Jack Heutel, Sunset Ford.

Maybe it is just me but there is a difference between "not bad" or "not too bad "and "good" or "OK." Get bad out of your vocabulary and you will have a happier life. I'm not saying overlook the obvious. But there are two ways to handle daily roadblocks. Either positive or negative.

The best attitude advise I ever got is "Fake it until you make it." Ric Middlekauff.

# CHAPTER 42

## MAXIMIZING FINANCE AND INSURANCE PROFITS

Years ago financing was just a convenience for the customer. Now is can be one of if not the most profitable part of the business. It requires no investment and can yield huge profits. It gives the sales department a source of control and creates instant profit.

The products are endless. Such things as warranties, protection packages, loss prevention systems, burglar alarms, credit life insurance, auto insurance, accident and health insurance and the list goes on and on are sold in the F&I office. These are all possible profit centers that are sold after the car.

Add the "spread" or finance reserve (the difference between what you pay for money and what it is sold at) and you have quite an opportunity to make serious profits on each vehicle sold.

There are limits however to what a customer can stand as far as after sell pressure. The F&I department is kind of like a pilot fish after a shark attack. If they are too aggressive they can blow the deal by over pressuring the client to buy their products. A good F&I manager walks a fine line trying to sell the added product lines.

As shown earlier, there are a lot of aftermarket product entries. I always felt that it is easier to concentrate on a few making fair margins rather than sell the whole line of products available. What usually sells the best is what the manager believes in the most. Some managers like alarms while others go for life policies. I was not that particular on what was sold as much as how much money I made on the average deal. One of the most important benchmarks in the store is your aftermarket profit per vehicle as compared to other dealers including finance reserve. If you are not in the top 20% someone needs training or another profession. Do not accept less.

The easiest way to make the most money is finance reserve, yet it is the hardest to keep because of refinancing and charge backs in early payoffs and repossessions. Profit is not obscene but just selling money to me is not morally right especially at some of the spreads I have seen over the years. It is also like play money in that you generally get credit for the profit, pay your employees on it, and then if the note is not paid in full, you have to give your profit back.

The vendors will let you know how you are doing in just about every line and try to get you to pay your people on their products. A car dealership is an open book of statistical analysis. Everyone has their nose in your business from the factory to the credit life vendor.

I'm not going to get into desking procedures, but the highest gross deals are sold by payments. There are three ways to sell a car. They are payments, difference and trade allowance. Profit comes from the markup on the vehicle plus the markup on the products sold in addition to the car including the markup on the money or finance reserve.

Profit can be spread in all sorts of creative ways depending how much of it you have and the products sold including the vehicle. It is important to keep a happy house because greed is a good and a bad thing. The sales man knows how much the finance manager makes and visa versa. There is usually a little friction between the departments, but it is essential that they work together to get the vehicle delivered for the highest reasonable profit.

.

# CHAPTER 43

## THE F&I TO!!!

Once a vehicle is sold to a customer, it needs to be sold to the finance source. To be sold to the finance source every deal needs to be presented properly. Usually the credit application is the source of personal information given to the credit company. Everyone from the sales man up at this point needs to assume that a banker is looking at each deal. Generally a car sales man does not take a good credit application!!

A finance deal can only be accepted, turned down, or conditioned. Many conditions however are just excuses for turndowns because the condition is so ridiculous it cannot be met. But every deal must be worked to the max for acceptance and full profit. Money talks and BS walks.

There is a saying that "YOU CAN ONLY GET WHAT YOU GOT.' It means that money down and trade equity determine the amount of profit you can make on a deal. Although this is not entirely true, if you keep this axiom in mind you will get more deals bought and make more profit.

The F&I TO means turn over. A change of face is a change of pace. If the F&I manager cannot get the deal bought and if there is any merit to the deal, the new car manager, general sales manager, general manager and even the dealer should be on the phone until the deal gets bought. You must also cultivate good relationships between the finance source and your employees. It is never a waste to give baseball tickets to your buyer.

# CHAPTER 44

## THE IMPORTANCE OF EXTENDED SERVICE CONTRACTS

There are numerous companies with extended service contract offerings. I prefer the Ford brand products or the brand backed by the manufacturer you represent. There are pros and cons to any product and if you represent several manufacturers than it probably makes more sense to go to a more universal product. Many very profitable dealers carry their own.

I guess I just believe in the value of the protection. As long as the customer wins and the dealer wins, it is a fair deal. The markup on service contracts can be very lucrative if sold properly.

Not only do you have a satisfied customer. But you have his service business, not if but when something breaks. You have the opportunity to have a customer for life.

The bottom line is to make sure your F&I people are selling service contracts building value and not just selling payments and loading the rate.

The first thing sold is the car. The second thing sold is the financing. And next is the service contract. After that it is what the market will bear.

## CHAPTER 45

TRIP-- Temporary Registration in Process.  Spot Deliveries

This is an old California acronym that is not heard in the Midwest, but its practices are well documented.  It is guaranteed to add 10% to your sales efficiency.

With today's information systems, it is something that most competitive dealers practice.  The more aggressive you are, the bigger the risk.  You must have competent management.  Many dealer's have the F&I department make the decision as to when to deliver the car.

The decision is whether or not to give possession of the vehicle to the buyer without having finance approval.   In many states if you give possession of the vehicle, the buyer cannot be prosecuted for theft if he does not bring the vehicle back if he is not accepted by the finance source.   The best document to use is a loan agreement for additional protection.

There are several advantages of delivering the vehicle "on the spot."  The biggest is it reduces buyer's remorse.  It reduces shopping.  It increases gross.  And increases sales.

Some disadvantages are:

1. The vehicle can be wrecked or damaged.

2. The vehicle might not be returned if the buyer cannot get financed.

3. The vehicle could get stolen.

Dealers should have written policies as to who makes the decision to "roll" a car. The first time I heard of this practice, the penalty for delivering a car recklessly was the manager who made the decision owned it. It was up to him to get it back or pay for it.

# CHATER 46

## Key Control

Believe it or not, but poor key control including misfiled and lost keys is a very big cause of lost deals.  A salesman only has so much quality time that a customer will allow.

It is 10 degrees outside.  The salesman has finally landed the customer on a car.  The customer wants to take a demonstration drive.  It is 9:30 PM and the dealership closes at 9 PM.  THE SALESMAN CANNOT FIND THE KEYS!!  The customer says "That's fine.  I'll come back tomorrow." In the morning the customer buys a car from another dealer.

It is Saturday afternoon in Austin, Texas in July, 4 PM.  It is 110 degrees outside and 130 inside the car. The salesman and the customer have looked at three cars and finally they want to drive the fourth. The keys are missing.  The customer says "I'll call you Monday."  That afternoon he drives to a competitor and drives his new truck home.

Most key problems come from inattentive sales management and salesmen.  It sounds trite and stupid, but do a key inventory of your lot. You will be surprised.

## CHAPTER 47

## WHAT IT COSTS TO PASS A DEAL

A lot of dealers require management to have an average gross per deal to enhance their profit. But does a higher gross per vehicle really increase profit? It may, but make sure you consider the following when reviewing how much money you lost by not selling a car because you did not make enough money on a particular deal. This is not a finite list, but you should get the point.

You lost a potential customer for life.

You lost the service business and warranty income potential.

You paid to get him in the door and wasted advertising money.

You did not have the opportunity for finance income.

You lost the opportunity for aftermarket sales.

If his trade was retailable, you lost used car profit.

You lost in most cases holdback.

You lost bragging rights and the intrinsic advertising that accompanies a new vehicle sale.

In my opinion the most important ratio, and believe me the factory ratios you to death, is your closing ratio. And 90% of dealers have no idea what that is.

The only time to have a gross per unit minimum is when the unit cannot be replaced such as a museum piece. And there are none of those in the car business.

It is imperative that you review individual deals with management. But if you overemphasize gross, you might get them passing deals to try to get their grosses higher.

# CHAPTER 48

## DON'T HIRE SALESMEN. HIRE CLOSERS

The sentences speak for themselves. Don't hire salesmen. Hire Closers. Earlier I discussed the 10 step selling procedure. That of course is a disciplined method to becoming a better salesman. The quality of a salesman depends on several factors. Most dealers would say money is the most important factor. The guy who makes the most money is my best salesman.

You know, what is crazy about the car business is there really is no standard pay plan in the industry and no standard for success measurement. Of course the bottom line is profit, but there are many other factors of success such as customer satisfaction which deals with long term success.

Getting back to closers--the best salesmen have a natural talent for knowing when to close the deal. I'm not too sure that intellect has much to do with it. A "natural born" salesman is not the gregarious loud pushy guy. The best just go about their way and seem to get the job done mostly without flash. They just have a natural aura of trust and the ability to get the order.

Naturally there are things one can do to improve themselves with various sales trainers, but many of the best just amaze me.

How do you hire them? I'm not sure. It seems they come along every once in awhile and when they do most owners are smart enough to realize it and do everything in their power to keep them.

## CHAPTER 49

## ABILTIY AND DESIRE

One of the first professional lectures I got after I started at Ford Marketing was from an executive comparing ability and desire. This lecture has stuck with me through out my career. I'm sure it applies to you in some fashion. The question is "Would you rather have a person with more ability or more desire?"

Basically it compares individuals with ability that wastes it vs. individuals with desire who do not have the ability. Give me the latter. It really has been a shame to see the talent I've seen over the years literally thrown away. And to see the number of people who really worked hard but could not master adequate selling skills. Many were successful, yet many failed.

Selling cars is not an easy job. I know of few dealerships that do not have a relatively large turnover. I really strived to hire people that I thought would be able to make a career out of this business vs. those hiring someone to sell their friends and relatives and move on. To me it is amazing how many dealerships do not care about longevity.

I do not think many people get a joy out of firing people and unfortunately it has to be done regularly in the automotive sales arena. Some people simply cannot close. Probably the best part is that you will generally know in 60 days if this business was meant for you.

There is always the third parameter, the individual who has both ability and desire.  It is a treat when you find one of those who are honest without personal problems.

However the solution to finding good people is rather simple. It depends on the dealer.  If he provides a good product with a competitive pay plan, good working conditions, inventory,
advertising and honesty they will flock to you.  You will need a elimination process vs. a searching process.  The best elimination processes are testing and interviewing.

## CHPTER 50

## TEN STEP SELLING

There are several terms for the road to a sale. Ten step, nine step, and it really doesn't matter as long as there is a method or guideline. This is a common sense approach to a sales system. We are creatures of habit. The more prepared one is the better the results will be.

Step 1. Greet. You just can't beat a warm friendly handshake and smile. Hello, my name is Fred. Welcome to Friendly Motors. Greet all the members of the party and repeat their names out loud. Write their names down on a 3X5 card and put it in your pocket. Next ask them how you can be of assistance.

Step 2. Sell yourself. Look good, feel good. Have a good attitude, walk tall, and take control. Ask open ended questions.

Step 3. Qualify. Ask questions. Who, what, where, when, why. Who is the driver? What is the main purpose for this vehicle? Is there a trade? Find this out early. Ask about payments if your manager allows it. Where have you been shopping?

Step 4. Land on vehicle. There are several schools of thought on this subject. One is take the customer to the inventory.. The other is to bring the vehicle to the client.

Step 5. Present the car. It is called a 6 point walk around. Start at the front and point out the features and benefits. End at the driver's door and show the interior. Have fun. Show them the trunk or rear area. Ask them to get in. Yes, even the trunk!

Step 6   Demonstration Drive.  Have a well planned demo route with as many right turns as possible.  Ask questions during this procedure.

Step 7.  Recap.  If the numbers are OK, is this the vehicle you would like to own?

Step 8.  Appraise the trade.

Step 9.  Close the deal, turn to F&I.

Step 10.  Follow up for future prospects.

# CHAPTER 51

## ORDER A WELL PLANNED INVENTORY

I spent two and a half years working for Ford Marketing in what was then called the distribution department, helping dealers order vehicles and scheduling them to be built at various assembly plants

The distribution process is complex and can make or cost a dealer serious money. Factories have been sued for millions of dollars for unfair distribution practices. Many dealers have just one person who does nothing but order vehicles and coordinate inventory.

Frank Bitter from San Antonio was a master at ordering vehicles. He had charts for color and option combinations. He spent days on his monthly order. Even today it is not an easy process.

The factory has representatives travel to dealerships and take monthly and weekly orders. But most of it is done over the computer. The factory has to build and sell vehicles. Because of lead time and market conditions the factory cannot meet exact market demands. Materials are preordered and lines take months and even years to change. Every vehicle that is planned to be built needs to be sold to a dealer.

So there is a constant battle between production the factory can build and what the consumer and dealers want. When we get unusual economic and unpredictable swings in demand the factory can have big problems. And factory problems become dealer problems even with the best of controls.

# CHAPTER 52

## THERE IS NO TOMMORROW

When I was green behind the ears as a field manager for Ford, my second territory was east Texas with Beaumont as the central area. There was a Ford dealer in Sour Lake that I was visiting for the first time. They were having a big sale and I was very excited to see the action.

He had pony rides, hay rides, free hotdogs, soda and balloons everywhere. Whenever something like this occurred upper management always liked to know so they could share successful ideas. I was excited and this dealer became one of my first heroes. I couldn't wait to notify to my boss about the excitement. They were a small dealership in a small town and selling cars and trucks like there was no tomorrow.

This was on a Thursday and I was on my way home to Houston eager to report the good news. I eagerly went into the district office and started bragging about this unbelievable sale one of my dealers was having.

Little did I know that while I was celebrating this huge success, Ford Motor Credit, his financial source, was padlocking his dealership as he was out of trust.

Monday morning I couldn't wait to get out into the field. I was going to beeline it straight to Sour Lake to see the results of this fantastic sale. I wanted to get to the dealership by noon to congratulate the dealer and take him to lunch.

When I got to the dealership, I could not believe my eyes. Everything was locked up. All the cars were gone. I thought I was in a dream.

There is not a happy ending to this story. I did find the dealer inside the store and we went to lunch. Unfortunately when these things go down, this is a pretty common scenario.

www.ingramcontent.com/pod-product-compliance
Lightning Source LLC
Chambersburg PA
CBHW071218200326
41519CB00018B/5578